Michael Jackson: The Making of "THRILLER"

4 Days/1983

Dedicated to the memory of the brilliance of Michael Jackson

"Are we not formed, as notes of music are,
For one another, though dissimilar?"

—Percy Bysshe Shelley

First published in the United States of America by
Hachette Filipacchi Media, U.S., Inc.
1633 Broadway
New York, NY 10019

First Edition

ISBN-13: 978-1-933231-98-3
Library of Congress Control Number: 2010921371

Conceived and produced by Glitterati Incorporated
www.Glitteratiincorporated.com
Design: Sarah Morgan Karp
Research: Beth Ackerman Bolander
Manufacturing: Lynn Scaglione

Printed in China

Shot with Kodakchrome and Ektachrome films
Dynalite strobes
Scans with Imacon/Hasselblad on Apple Mac computers
Proofing with HP Z3200 printers and Legion and HP papers

Michael Jackson: The Making of "THRILLER"
4 Days/1983

Douglas Kirkland
with an Introduction by Nancy Griffin

CONTENTS

The Story Of "THRILLER"

On a dark and eerie night, Michael Jackson and a young woman are seen together in a car that Michael is driving, when they stop outside a wooded area to take a romantic walk. Michael gives the girl a ring and explains that he is unlike any other fellow; but the girl explains that this is why she likes him! Michael says emphatically that she doesn't understand him: that he really is different from other boys. As he is explaining this, the full moon appears. . . Michael hides his face and the girl asks him why he is doing this. When he looks back at her his face has changed! He is suddenly looking like an animal, covered in hair, with elongated eyes and teeth like a wolf. He's becoming a werewolf! He pushes the girl away as she screams, and she turns and runs. Michael the werewolf chases her; she stumbles and falls and when Michael reaches her, he is a werewolf.

Suddenly the scene changes to a crowded movie theater where Michael and his girlfriend are watching a werewolf film. The girl is terrified; Michael enjoys it. The girlfriend is too frightened to stay so she gives Michael her popcorn and leaves the theatre. Michael goes after her and when he catches up with her outside, it's clear she doesn't like horror films. But Michael seems relaxed as he stands in front of the theatre marquis that reads, "Thriller."

As the pair walks through the deserted streets, passing a cemetery, Michael is teasing his girlfriend for being afraid of a mere film. She tells him she was

not afraid, but he keeps taunting her, dancing around her in circles. All of a sudden, zombies start to emerge from the darkness, climbing out from their tombs in the cemetery. Within moments they have surrounded the pair. Now the girl realizes that Michael is one of them. . . Michael and the zombies dance in tandem.

The girl races to a nearby abandoned house, flying up the stairs and slamming doors behind her for protection. But the zombies have followed her and suddenly they have broken through into the room where she is hiding. They move toward her and it looks as if she may be totally in their control.

A new scene suddenly: The girl wakes up in the same room of the same house as the one that appeared in her nightmare, but it seems it must have all been a horrifying nightmare. No one except her boyfriend is in the room with her and Michael calms her and tells her she is safe, although they must now leave. As they leave, Michael looks at the camera with his yellow eyes; clearly these are not "human" eyes.

As the video comes to a close, the zombies are returning to their tombs in the cemetery and the worst of the group scowls at the camera. Who knows what has happened here?

INTRODUCTION

Nancy Griffin

For Douglas Kirkland and me, this book represents a bittersweet look back. Twenty-seven years ago, we worked as a photographer-writer team covering the making of Michael Jackson's "Thriller" video for *Life* magazine. Recently we got together to recall our experiences on the set. Although we have logged in some eighty combined years working as entertainment journalists, we agreed that neither of us had ever—nor have we since—been in the presence of a greater talent than Michael Jackson.

Back then, Michael's capacity for dazzling audiences seemed limitless. What we could not have known is that "Thriller" would represent the peak of both his artistry and his personal life. While he would remain the biggest star in the world for a decade and produce more remarkable music, videos and live shows, he was ultimately unable to cope with the harsh scrutiny his superstardom brought. What had seemed like youthful eccentricities became more pronounced and debilitating. In a metaphorical sense, the dark fears and fantasies Jackson expressed in "Thriller" came true. Whether he was victim or perpetrator in his later years we may never know. What we know for sure is that his life was complicated and he did not find happiness. It is impossible to reconcile the troubled, disfigured person Michael became with the radiant young man we knew. And now he is gone too soon.

The shrieks and squeals of fans straining at police barricades cascaded over us on a cold October night in 1983 as Douglas and I approached the Palace Theater, which bore the title *Thriller* on its marquis, in deserted downtown Los Angeles. Everyone involved with the production had been sworn to secrecy and security was tight, but word had leaked out and the fans showed up.

The crew was hurriedly making final adjustments to lights and cameras for the scene where Jackson and his "date," actress Ola Ray, emerge from the theater where they have just watched a scary movie. Jackson's parents, Joseph and Katherine, and his sister La Toya sat watching from directors' chairs nearby. The star himself was standing in the theater's entryway in his red leather jacket with black stripes, laughing and clowning with director John Landis and Ola Ray. Judging by the saucy looks she was sending in his direction, Ray seemed smitten by her leading man, who responded by casually throwing an arm around her shoulders. I saw Douglas discreetly move in and fire off some frames of the pair. Landis asked me if I'd be willing to appear in the background of the scene and before I knew it, I was sitting in the ticket booth.

"How are you going to be in this shot?" Landis shouted to Jackson, just before calling "action!"

"Wonderful," he replied.

Which, of course, the whole world now knows he was. When the cameras rolled, Jackson looked like a matinee idol, glowing and confident, as he smiled and reassured Ola Ray that "it's only a movie." On a later night we would see Jackson unleash his full power, when the young suitor he played

turned into a ghoul and danced with a group of zombies. Jackson was, simply, breathtakingly fluid as he executed the fabulously funky footwork he had created with choreographer Michael Peters. We watched, agape, as he slithered and jerked to a playback version of the song that had been remixed for the video.

When we were given the run of the set for four days, Douglas and I recognized that it was a special undertaking. No entertainer had yet mounted such a costly music video (half a million dollars, shot on 35mm film) or collaborated with a feature director such as Landis (*Animal House; The Blues Brothers*). The fourteen-minute short film won multiple awards, including a Grammy. *The Guinness Book of World Records* lists it as the most popular video of all time. But the global reverberations of "Thriller"—today thousands of fans from Manila to Melbourne to Mexico City don ghoulish make-up and break out into public "zombie dances," copying Michael's moves—have far surpassed anyone's wildest imaginings.

Douglas and I testified to one of the most triumphant, game-changing moments in show business history. In the early 1980s Michael Jackson had emerged as a solo artist, rejecting his father's domination and shedding his image as the precocious child singer of The Jackson 5, with his hit album *Off the Wall*. Then he dropped a bomb on the recording industry with his *Thriller* album, which with sales of twenty-five million and counting was on its way to becoming the biggest-selling record of all time. With that album Jackson achieved his lifelong ambition: to become the most popular entertainer on the planet. He heralded a new world order when he unveiled the moonwalk during his electrifying performance of "Billie Jean" on Motown's televised 25th anniversary celebration, in front of such childhood idols as Marvin Gaye, Stevie Wonder and Diana Ross.

Photographer Douglas Kirkland captures journalist Nancy Griffin with Michael on the set before the shooting begins.

With his universally appealing style, Jackson radically rearranged the pop culture landscape. He called everyone to the dance floor with his exuberant musical melange, dissolving racial barriers that had long divided audiences for disco, funk, rock, and synth. His videos for "Billie Jean" and "Beat It" were the first clips by a black artist to go into heavy rotation on the fledgling MTV network, creating a hot commercial market for music videos and paving the way for other artists such as Prince.

"Michael and MTV rode each other to glory," said *Thriller*'s producer, Quincy Jones. One night while visiting the set Jones admitted to me, as we watched Jackson dance, that he was more stunned than anyone by the album's phenomenal popularity.

The twenty-five-year-old star was creatively on fire and canny about his career. It was Jackson who concocted the werewolf-on-a-date concept for his album's third video. After six months of dominating the charts and six hit singles, the record's sales had begun to flag, which dismayed Jackson. Having seen Landis' comedic-horror flick, *An American Werewolf in London*, Jackson called the director and asked him to create a narrative short film that would turn him into a monster. The video had to be funny as well as spooky, because "I never was a horror fan," Jackson said. "I was too scared. I liked Vincent Price." Quincy Jones had drafted Price to narrate the "funk of forty thousand years" rap at the song's end.

The script called for Michael to appear in three distinct incarnations: normal eighties Michael, Michael as a fifties guy on a date who turns into a werewolf (including the requisite "transformation" shot), and a ghoul who boogies down with his undead posse. A few nights after the Palace Theater scene, the production was ensconced in a wooded section of Griffith Park, with Michael in front of the cameras in a red baseball jacket and full werewolf make-up. Landis was coaching him on how to act like a fearsome beast, which was a stretch for the soft-spoken, ninety-nine-pound star. The director demonstrated how he wanted Jackson to lunge and growl at Ola Ray as she shrieked in terror.

"Go get her!" he prompted. "She looks delicious. Rrrrr!"

The yellow contact lenses Jackson was wearing hurt, and he winced between takes.

Make-up impresario Rick Baker had been given creative latitude in designing Jackson's look, and veered it toward a werecat rather than a werewolf.

"Because it was Michael, we couldn't go for a standard monster," he explained. "His face lends itself very well to this make-up. He's got such a gaunt face, with high cheekbones and expressive eyes."

Michael adored the make-up effects and calmly endured long hours in Baker's chair; his foot tapped constantly, as Douglas documented the process. For the werecat, a latex foam mask with yak hair whiskers was glued to his skin; ears and hairpieces were attached; false teeth were fitted over his own teeth; and paws with long claws slipped over his hands.

"If even a small portion of the praise that is bestowed on Michael Jackson now was given to him last year in life he might well still be with us. That is the sad truth. One consolation is that he will triumph by his legacy."

—Robin Gibb
Bee Gees, singer-songwriter

"It's not uncomfortable at all," Michael said of the make-up, except for the yellow contacts.

One day as he sat in the make-up chair, an assistant arrived carrying a yellow pillowcase. Michael reached in and pulled out Muscles, his pet boa constrictor. Later that day on a break he approached me with an impish grin. He gently wrapped the snake around my neck.

"Don't worry, Muscles won't hurt you," he murmured. His voice was so whispery, I had to lean in to hear him.

Throughout his career Jackson's burning ambition to be the greatest kept him focused on his legacy. He once quoted Michelangelo as saying "know the creator will go, but his work survives. That is why, to escape death, I attempt to bind my soul to my work. And that's how I feel. I give my all to my work. I just want it to live."

And "Thriller" does live. The photographs in this book freeze the incandescent moment when a young black man from Gary, Indiana, rocketed to super-stardom. Douglas Kirkland has captured Michael Jackson in all his brilliance, giving his all to his artistry. From the time he was a boy it was Michael's aim above all other things to transmit the joy he felt when he was singing and dancing. This was his gift to all of us, and it was huge and heartfelt. His music and his moves are eternal.

Q&A with Douglas Kirkland

Nancy Griffin
and Douglas Kirkland

Nancy: Do you recall your first impressions of Michael?

Douglas: I met him for the first time on the night they were shooting at the Palace Theater, when I was taken to meet him in his trailer. Frankly I was somewhat intimidated at first. I've been around a lot of people, but I had no idea what kind of individual he would be. He already had so much myth surrounding him. I wondered if he was going to be strange or odd—who was this person I was going to be with, and how could I best do my job?

With the power that Michael Jackson demonstrated on stage, and the aura that had been created around him, I expected him to behave like an assured giant in dealing with a *Life* magazine photographer and journalist.

What I found was somebody who wasn't remotely threatening or intimidating. In fact, he was disarming, and very responsive. He made me feel at home. He had a small voice and smiled easily, not a big smile but a small smile. A very light handshake as I recall, not a firm, "I'm in charge," kind of handshake at all.

Everything about him made me think that he was a gentle person.

Did his shyness affect the way you approached photographing him?

I was concerned that I didn't want to be too loud, and I wanted to be polite. I always have my senses very acutely tuned so as not to overstep or assume too much. In those few minutes I tried to show my respect for him.

As a person taking pictures I quickly try to drift into the background; the hellos are just to warm everything up. It worked because he was very receptive.

I remember he was hanging out in front of the theater before they started shooting. He struck me as shy but friendly, and surprisingly accessible.

When I went into his trailer he was having his make-up done, and he was actually ready before the crew was. He came out and was sitting outside the theater in a director's chair talking to everyone. They had a video pinball machine there, and I have pictures of him playing with it.

Michael was playing a cute young guy out on a date with a pretty girl. John Landis made sure Michael was dressed and lit to look sexy, like a movie star.

He was so good-looking. I look very carefully at people and right away I thought 'this is very cool, because I have a good-looking subject and if he doesn't have attitude this is going to work.'

Did you ask Michael to pose or do anything special?

No, I did what I typically like to do when I start working with someone, which is come in very quietly and photograph what I'm observing. I feel that that is a time for them to get comfortable with me being around. The most I would ask Michael for at first was "could you turn this way for a second?" As the days and evenings progressed, I was more inclined to ask for special favors.

Did he seem knowledgeable about your work or photography in general?

Frankly, to him I think I just represented *Life* magazine. John Landis and everyone else involved with "Thriller" was very pleased that *Life* was there. I didn't get the impression that Michael knew a great deal about photography, and he didn't say anything about it. I heard that he collected antique cameras, but he didn't know what my 300mm f2.8 lens was, what it represented or why I would have that piece of equipment. It's what I used to take interesting pictures of him in close-up from a distance.

You weren't standing near him when you shot close-ups?

No, I took pictures with a long lens when he was sitting in his chair. I had a flash on him because he was in the dark. There's one of him in profile biting his tongue, and a light in the distance forms a kind of bubble behind his face. I was shooting with 64 Kodachrome film—everything was 35mm, it was a pre-digital film—which sadly is no longer made.

The portraits you captured that first night when he was acting with Ola, before he was transformed into a werewolf or a zombie, are quite glamorous.

When he stepped out into the motion picture lights and was preparing to perform—that's when his star quality could really be seen. In those minutes just before shooting, I was watching and following him with my long lens. This rather shy individual suddenly radiated confidence. He projected this glorious smile which could warm anybody up. My favorite pictures of him have this smile. That was Michael being Michael, and that's when I made my best pictures. He was in this beautiful lighting, the motion picture tungsten lights, so I used a fast Ektachrome 160 tungsten film. *TIME* magazine commissioned Andy Warhol to interpret one of those portraits for its cover. And years later I put one in my book, *Freeze Frame*.

Ola Ray looked like she had a crush on him.

I saw that, too. What a waste! (laughs) This beautiful girl, who obviously really did like him. And had he just dropped a penny in her direction, it was a *fait accompli*, it would have been a done deal. But he wasn't wired that way.

We were really watching history being made: The Thriller *album had redefined pop music, and now Michael was jump-starting the music video revolution.*

Director Sidney Lumet recalls that his teenage daughters had friends over and one asked Michael to sing: "I think he was embarrassed by the closeness of the situation, but his desire not to be rude or hurt led him to say 'yes.'"

This was such an innovative period for him, it was tremendously exciting. He had broken away from The Jackson 5 and taken control of his career. He looked so great, he had such extraordinary ability, and watching him perform in "Thriller" or when he unveiled the moonwalk at the Motown 25th anniversary show, I felt that he wanted to explode, and do his best. He was still searching for who he was as a performer, and what he reached for he accomplished, and did it brilliantly.

Michael said that he had never really liked horror movies, but he enjoyed An American Werewolf in London *because it mixed comedy into the horror.*

He got together with John Landis and they created "Thriller" and had such fun with it. It was landmark; it established what a music video could be— more than someone just standing there playing a guitar. It was telling a story, like a small feature film. At that time the narrative video hadn't been invented, and everybody copied it afterwards and it changed music videos forever.

I remember him sitting for hours in Rick Baker's chair getting the monster make-up applied.

It was a long process, and it was dreadfully uncomfortable for him. They put yellow contact lenses in his eyes, which were hard to see through, and they hurt. He was amused looking in the mirror. I also remember at the end of the night the glue they used to apply the mask had to be torn off and in some of the pictures you can see his pain; it was like someone pulling bandages off his face. But he was very good-natured about it. I don't remember him snapping at anyone. I never saw one bit of resistance; I never saw anybody get yelled at.

He'd been in show business for so long, he was a real pro.

Without a doubt. He knew why he was there, why people like you and I were there. There was no naiveté about any of it. He was well-prepared to do the role. "Thriller" was so well-produced, it was like a fine machine.

The shot of Michael as a ghoul reaching toward you was one of the only non-candid photos you took. How did it happen?

I had the idea of *him* spooking *me*, as if he were going to strangle me, in this madness that he was living in as a werewolf. It was a day when they were working at Raleigh Studios on ghoul scenes. I asked Michael if he would be willing to do the photograph and he said he would when he could, but that he had to stand by for shooting. I waited, and I was conscious that the sun was going down. Finally we got permission to go outside behind the soundstage. An assistant director came with us in case they needed Michael on the set in a hurry.

The job of the camera is to frame up what I've seen in my mind's eye and put it into the box, so to speak. The light was perfect and I got Michael into position so I could shoot right away. I was using a strobe light on him with

my shutter speed down to ⅛ of a second to get the dimming sky behind him in the picture. The lens was a wide angle 28 to 50mm. We probably spent five minutes, maximum, together. I pretty much knew what I needed, what I wanted to get. I work quickly because there is always a clock ticking, especially with stars.

I said, "Michael, I want to be frightened by you. You are the werewolf— scare the hell out of me!?"

He did this maybe three times, putting his hands out towards me menacingly, then reaching up towards the sky. I pushed him with words as I was shooting to get him to intensify his expression. That is one of secrets behind making this kind of photography—then you must be ready to catch the moment and not let it slip away.

There are so many things going on in a photographer's head at this point: focus, shutter speed, aperture, framing, light, how many exposures of film you have left. In those critical few seconds, my heart rate goes way up. All the while I am talking to the subject to keep his focus on me and my camera. It's not for my ego, it's for the purpose of getting the best image. When Michael was on the set I was observing and trying to extract the best *image,* but here I was creating the *picture.* Michael was giving himself to me completely, and I had to make sure that I was getting it with no technical errors.

One of Michael's strongest early influences was Diana Ross, who befriended him when The Jackson 5 first joined Motown. He adored her. You worked for many years with Diana—did she ever talk about Michael?

I did most of Diana's photography for about a ten-year period, before the "Thriller" video was made. She would periodically speak of Michael in a very warm way. She had real admiration and affection for him—her eyes would light up every time that she spoke about him.

Of all the entertainers you've been around, is there any one that Jackson reminds you of?

I've photographed a lot of people, and seen some geniuses. Peter Sellers was a genius: he had a way of knowing what buttons to press, what to do to create an impression, make people laugh and enjoy themselves. Michael wasn't a comedian, but he had a comparable quality of knowing how to get the most out of a performance. People who aren't in or around show business don't realize that the spontaneity they see has to be carefully created. Michael could "light up" for people when he was going before the lens, and really project a personality and a joy or whatever was necessary.

Did you get upset seeing what happened in later years with Michael after the "Thriller" video was shot?

Yeah, well Michael Jackson's life since the days we knew him has made me sad in many ways. Like a lot of people, I would get impatient with him, thinking, 'he's got all the money in the world, why can't he pull himself together?'

I don't know how people feel about what he did with his face, and his whole lifestyle. But he was trying to make himself a life, that's why he had children, I'm sure. He was trying to live some sort of normal life the only way he knew how. And unfortunately I don't think he did very well. Life ultimately was not good to him. As a kid with The Jackson 5, it's no secret that the father was very hard on him.

After seeing the movie This Is It, I believe that he would have achieved a comeback.

I do, too. I did not know what to expect when I went to see it. I really enjoyed it, and I could see the continuation of where he was on "Thriller." Certainly he was older; he didn't have the youth in his face any more and his appearance had been corrupted by what he did to it over the years. But once he started to perform he was magnetic; he still moved in that beautiful fluid way.

And what I was pleased about was that all the problems he had that we knew about, whatever happened at Neverland—it didn't matter to me. My belief is that Michael Jackson was a child when I knew him, a talented child. And when I saw the last film I felt that he had remained a child; that's who he was. I found that pleasing, watching him rehearse. He was a child and I think he was living in a child's fantasy. Part of his development was arrested in some way. It may have been a result of the way he was raised.

And the genius was still there. It's tragic that the curtain has dropped on this superb, brilliant performer. When Michael caught the beat, he danced with such absolute, refined perfection. I don't think it's ever been done as well before. And it may never be again.

Outside The Palace

"Michael Jackson was not an artist who comes along once in a decade, a generation, or a lifetime. He was an artist who comes along only once, period. He was the consummate student. He studied the greats and became greater. He raised the bar and then BROKE the bar."

—Berry Gordy
From the introduction of the
Michael Jackson memoir *Moonwalk*

"John Landis recognizes the approaching figure and Michael is star-struck as he shakes Rock Hudson's hand. Marc Christian looks on."

—Douglas Kirkland

"Originally, when I did my 'Thriller' demo, I called it 'Starlight.' Quincy said to me, 'You managed to come up with a title for the last album, see what you can do for this album.' I said, 'Oh great,' so I went back to the hotel, wrote two or three hundred titles, and came up with the title 'Midnight Man.' The next morning, I woke up, and I just said this word. . . Something in my head just said, this is the title. You could visualize it on the top of the Billboard charts. You could see the merchandising for this one word, how it jumped off the page as 'Thriller.'

"When I wrote 'Thriller,' I'd always envisioned this talking section at the end and didn't really know what we were going to do with it. But one thing I'd thought about was to have 'somebody,' a famous voice in the horror genre, to do this vocal. Quincy's [then] wife [Peggy Lipton] knew Vincent Price so Quincy said to me, 'How about if we got Vincent Price?' and I said, 'Wow, that'd be amazing if we could get him. . .'"

—**Rod Temperton**
Lyricist and songwriter

The "Thriller" video won for Best Performance Video, Best Choreography, and Viewer's Choice at the first MTV Video Music Awards in 1984.

" . . . but with his iconic signature steps like the moonwalk and all of his spins and side glides, that was just in his body. That was innate. That's the stuff you do without thinking about it. . . "

—Travis Payne
Associate producer of *This Is It*

Creating the Make-up for
Michael's Werewolf

"John told me about the idea but I was reluctant. I got a call from John (Landis) and he was like, 'You know who Michael Jackson is?' and I was like, 'Yeah, kinda. He's the guy from The Jackson 5, right?' And he said, 'Well he's got this song called "Thriller" and he wants to do this short film.' At first I said I didn't want to do it. It's not a popular job—it's like being a dentist in a way: they have to sit still in a chair for hours while you work on them, it's uncomfortable—it's not something actors look forward to.

"You start with the casting of the actor's face, then the latex, the contact lenses. . . Michael's make-up started more as a werewolf and then became more cat-like. Normally you would make a cast of every actor's face, but we'd only have three days from meeting the dancers to finishing their faces, so we couldn't do it that way. I wasn't too happy about that, but in the end we made three sizes of zombie mask. We couldn't do the teeth how we normally would, either. I suggested that myself [sic] and the crew be zombies, so that we could have a few that were done properly—because we could have more time to work on the make-up.

"Michael was great and very shy. I remember the first time John came over to shoot us working on Michael's make-up for his behind-the-scenes stuff— which I wasn't too happy about and Michael wasn't too happy about— Michael was so nervous that, as soon as the cameras came in, he ran off and hid in the bathroom. So different to when he was performing—"Thriller" was happening during the making of the Motown Anniversary Special, when Michael first did the moonwalk, and one of the guys brought a tape of the show in and and said, 'Watch this.' That was him, when he was performing; that was when he came alive."

—**Rick Baker**
Make-up effects

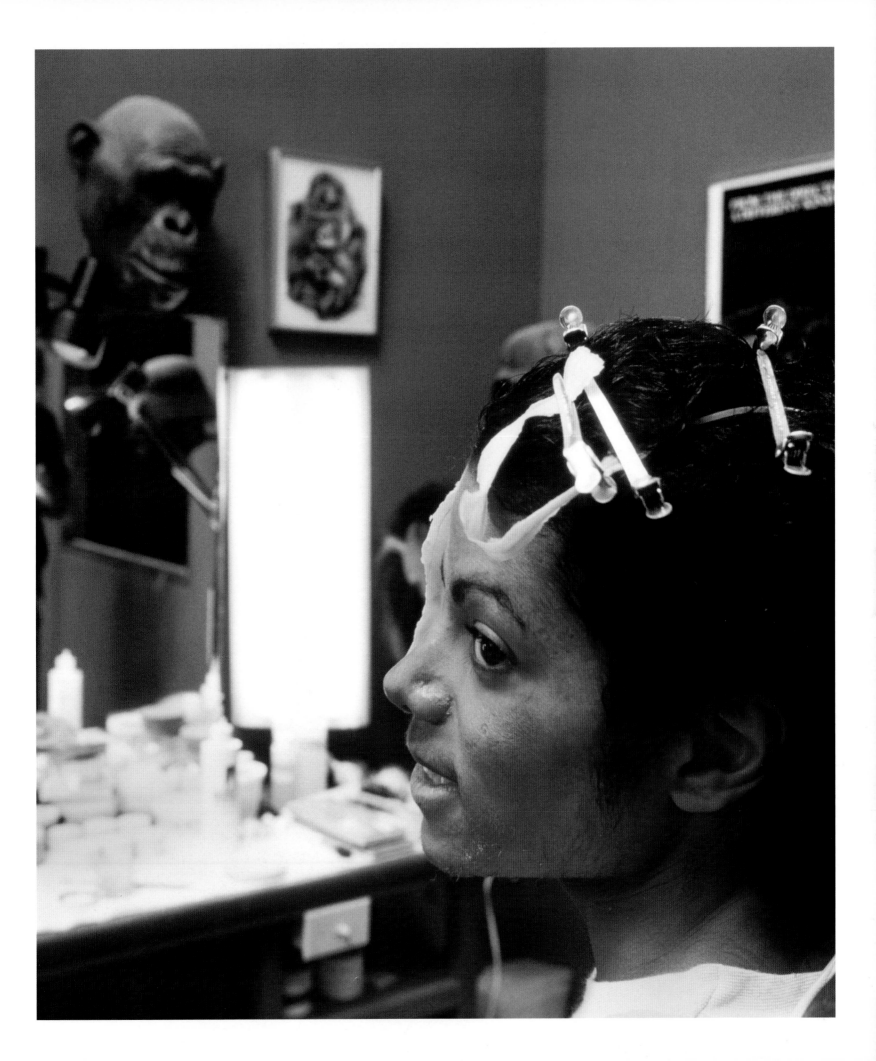

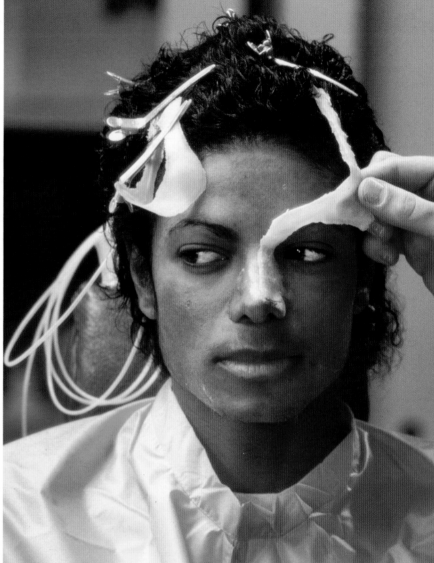

"What is a genius? What is a megastar? Michael—that's all. And when you think you know him, he gives you more. I think he is one of the finest people to hit this planet, and in my estimation, he is the true King of Pop, Rock, and Soul."

—Elizabeth Taylor
Actress

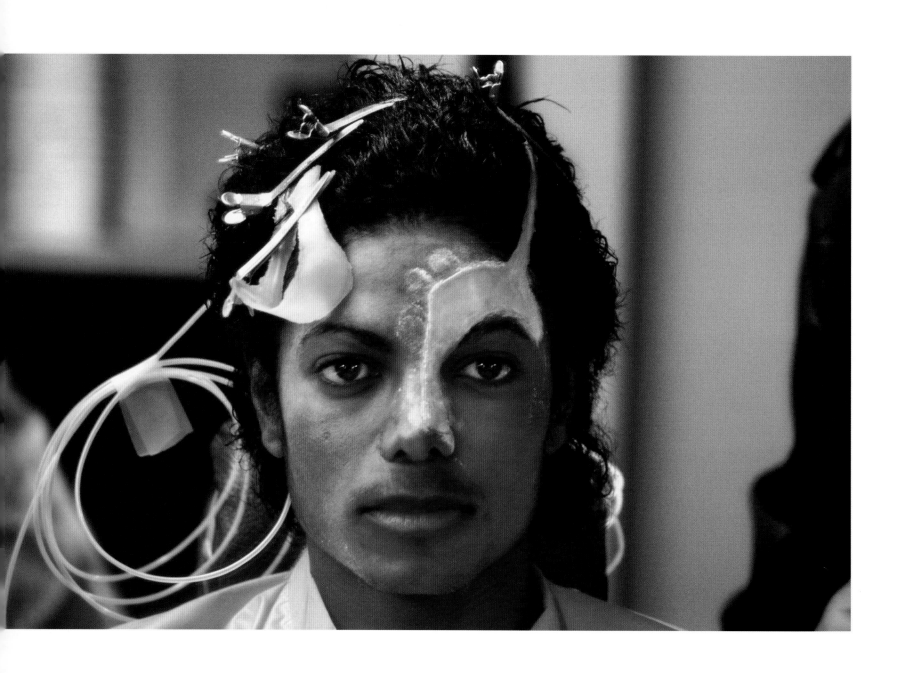

"Michael Jackson is the reason why I do music and why I am an entertainer. I continue to be humbled and inspired by his legacy. . . No one will ever be better."

—Chris Brown
Singer, songwriter, actor

 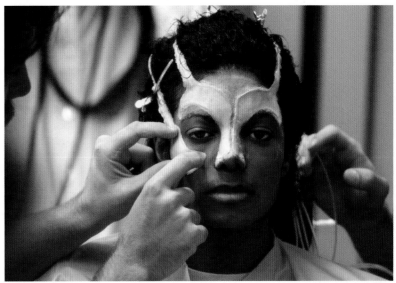

"I recall Michael sitting on a chair, in [his] bedroom, staring at the television, watching the 1980 Grammy awards show crying . . . because [he] had won only one Grammy award; and he said, 'Watch, La Toya, my next record, I am going to sell more records and win more Grammys than anyone in the history of music. . . I will be the biggest and the greatest entertainer of all time.'"

—La Toya Jackson
Musician, television personality, Michael's sister

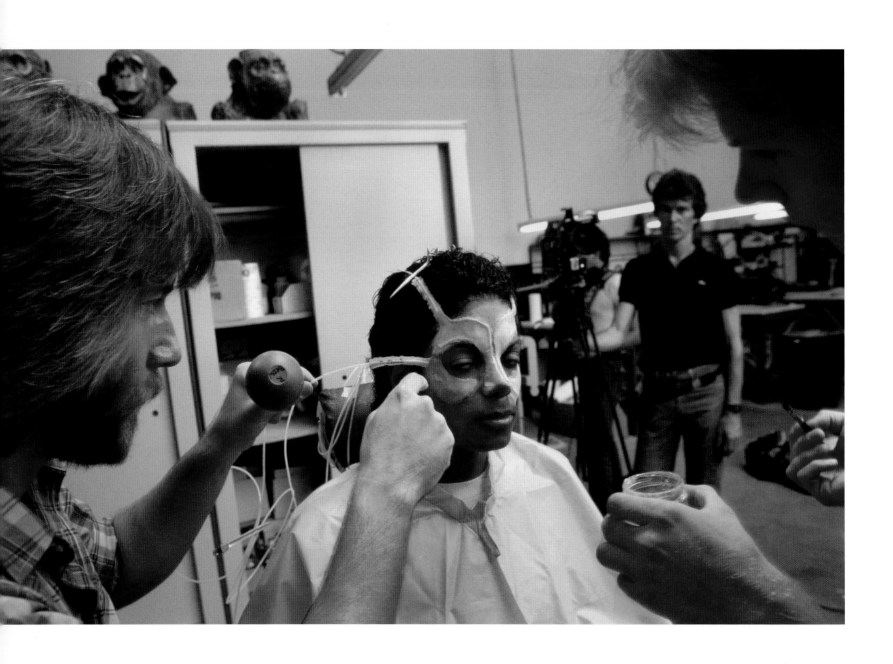

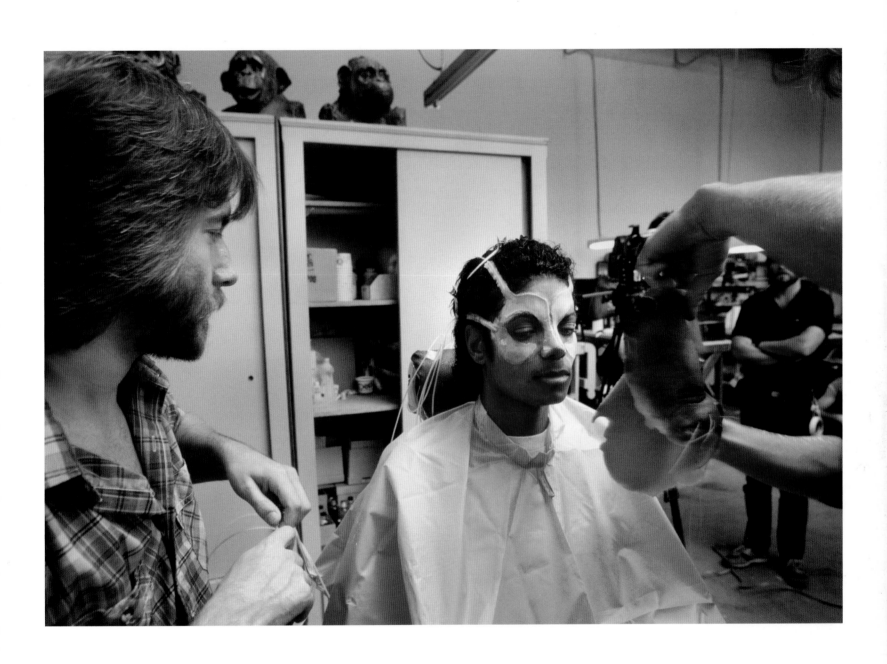

"He wasn't ever really interested in money. I'd give him his share of a night's earnings and the next day he'd buy ice cream or candy for all the kids in the neighborhood."

—Joe Jackson
Michael's father

"It's difficult to hear the songs from *Thriller* and disengage them from the videos. For most of us the images define the songs. In fact it could be argued that Michael is the first artist of the MTV age to have an entire album so intimately connected in the public imagination with its imagery."

—Nelson George
Music critic, journalist

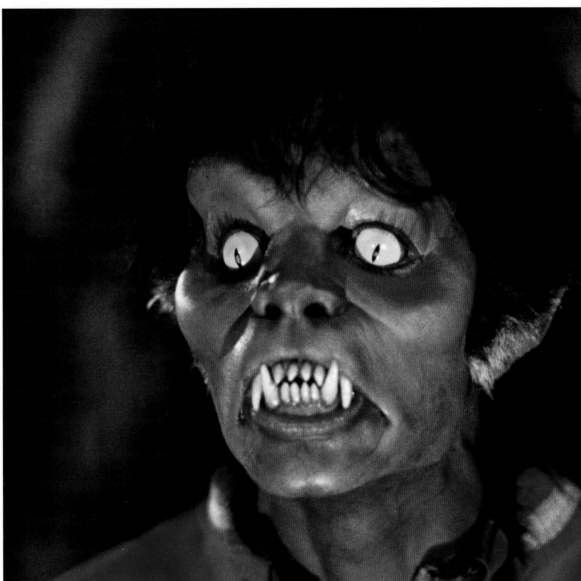

"He's taken us right up there where we belong. Black music had to play second fiddle for a long time, but its spirit is the whole motor of pop. Michael has connected with every soul in the world."

—Quincy Jones
Producer of *Thriller*

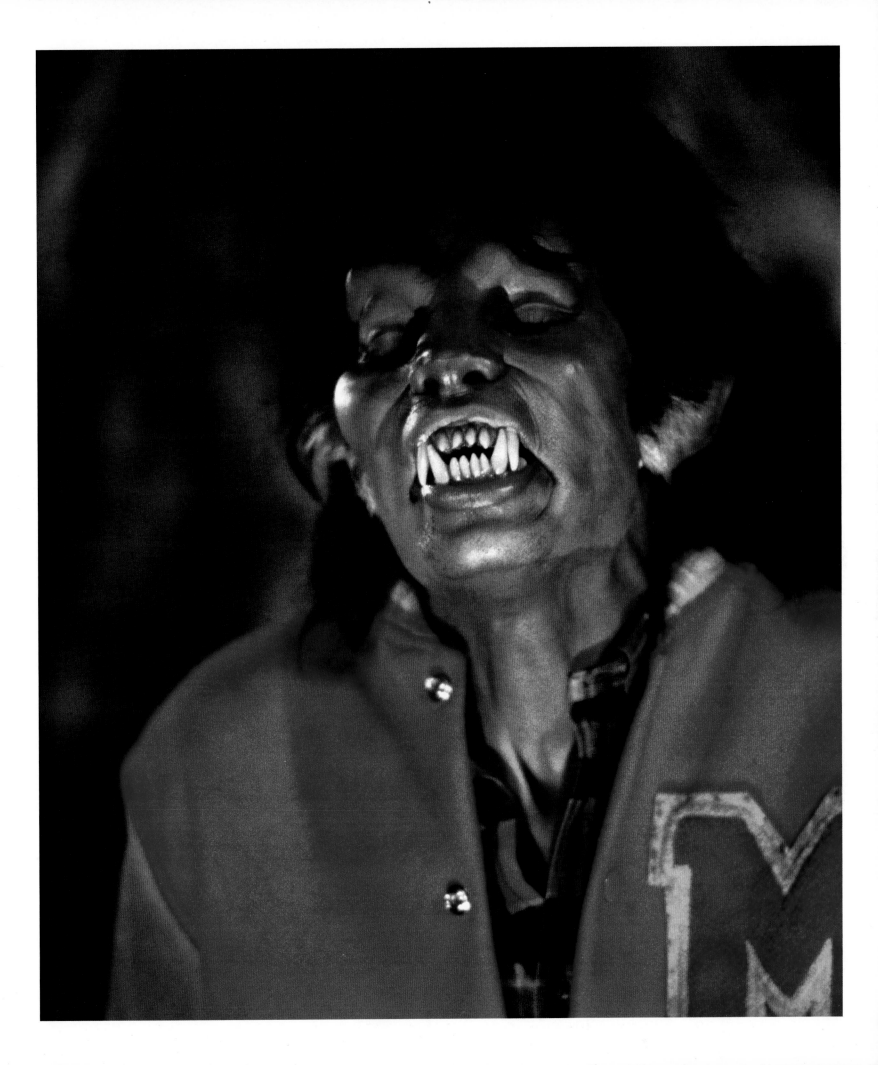

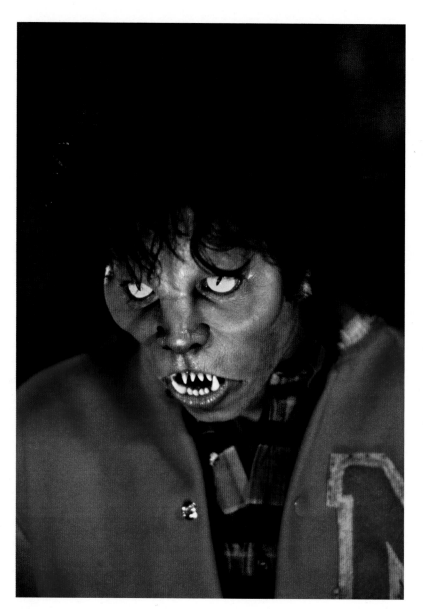 

" Michael Jackson will live forever through the thing that he put all of his life energy into: his music."

—Ne-Yo
Songwriter, musician

"If E.T. hadn't come to Elliot, he would have come to Michael's house. I think Michael can be hurt very easily; he's sort of like a fawn in a burning forest."

—Steven Spielberg
Film director, producer, screenwriter

" [Michael was] a genius and a true ambassador of not only pop music but of all music. He has been an inspiration to multiple generations and I will always cherish the moments I shared with him on stage and all of the things I learned about music from him and the time we spent together."

—Justin Timberlake
Musician, producer, actor

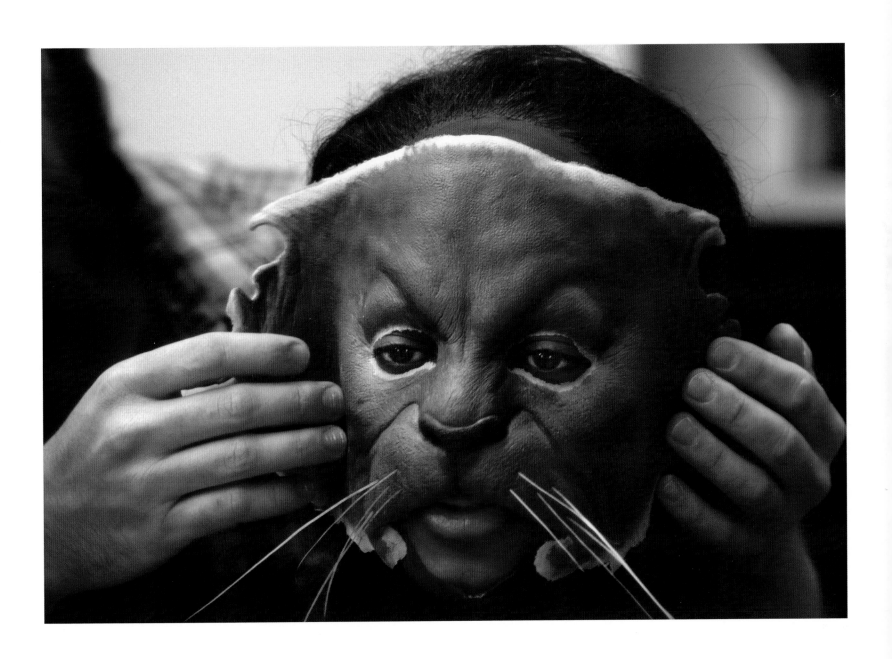

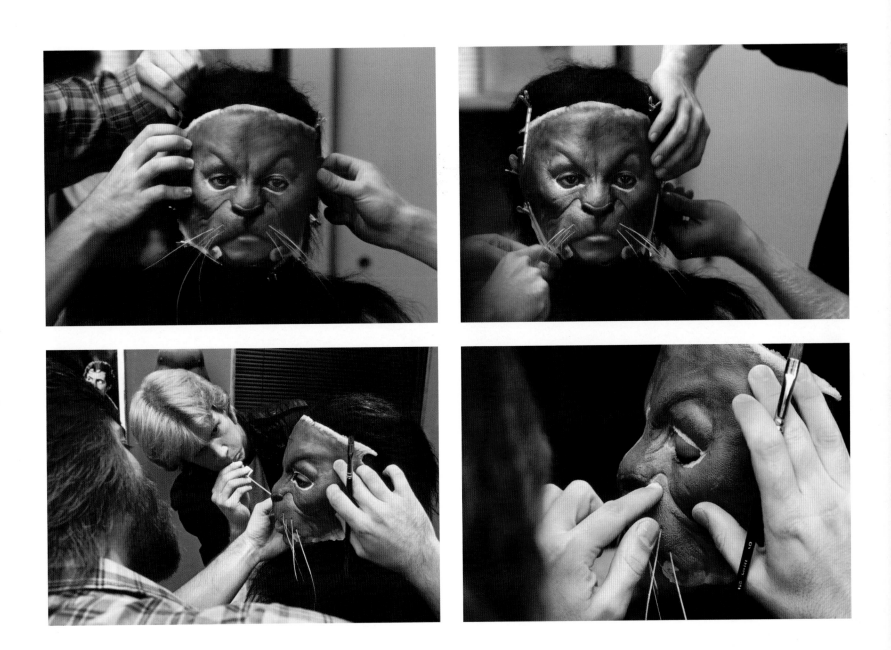

" MICHAEL JACKSON the first 2 english words i eva spoke. The future sucx!"

—M.I.A.
Singer-songwriter, rapper, record producer

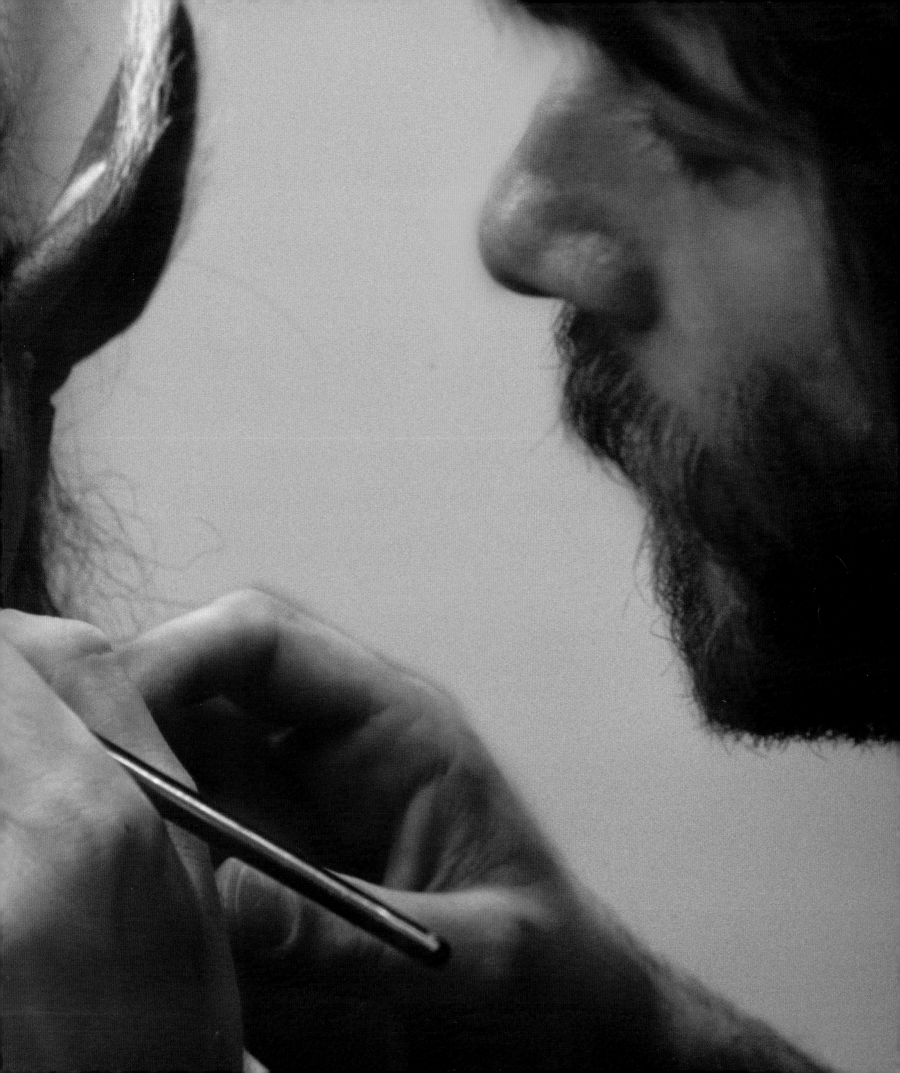

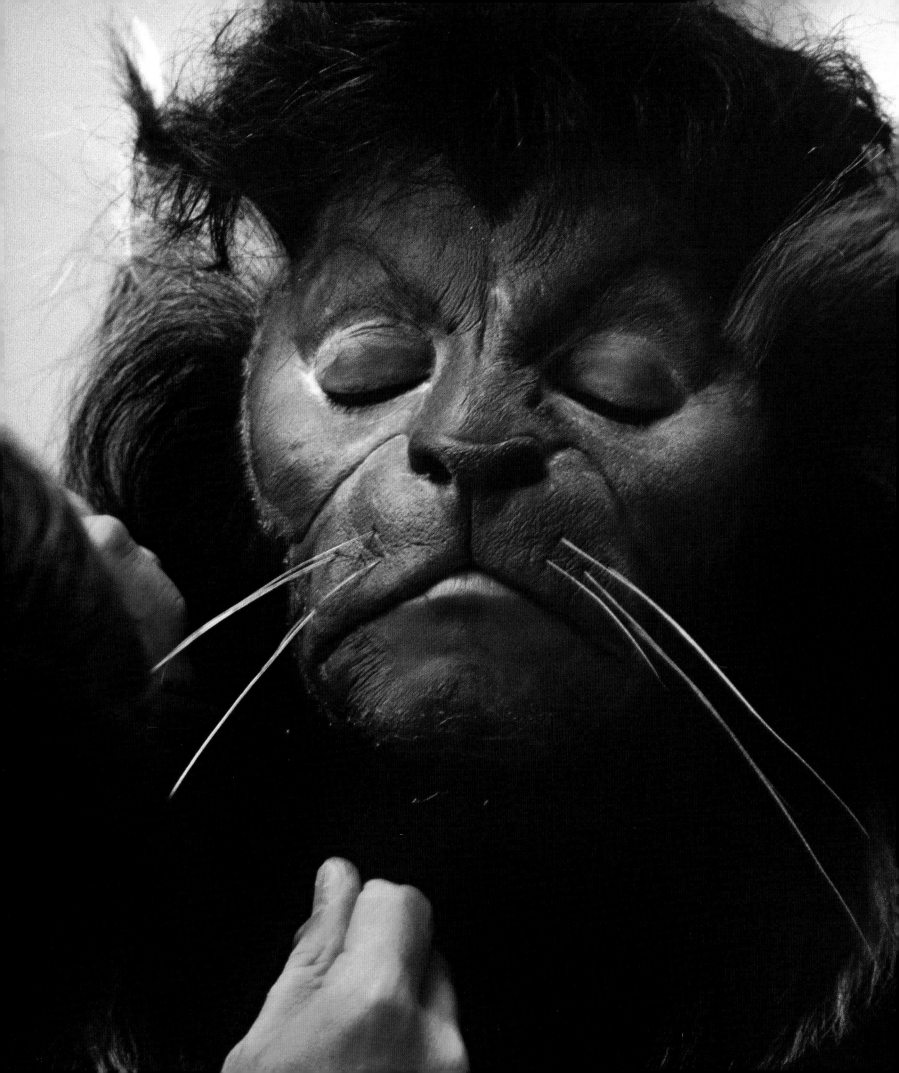

 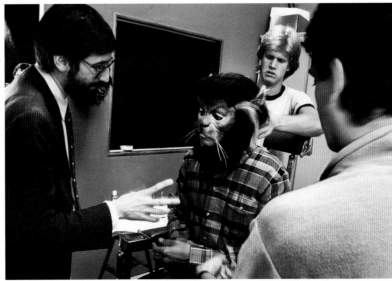

" . . . if it was shiny, if it had any kind of bling, he loved it. It was that drummer boy look. Do you remember that black jacket he wore for Motown's 25th anniversary? That's our mother's! He grabbed it from her closet! He loved anything that sparkled."

—Janet Jackson
Musician, producer, actress, Michael's sister

"Academy Award-winning make-up artist Rick Baker spends endless hours perfecting all aspects of Michael Jackson's make-up from head to toe."

—Douglas Kirkland

Different:
The 1950s Werewolf "Thriller"

"To this day, the music we created together on *Off the Wall*, *Thriller* and *Bad* is played in every corner of the world and the reason for that is because he had it all . . . talent, grace, professionalism and dedication. He was the consummate entertainer and his contributions and legacy will be felt upon the world forever. I've lost my little brother . . . , and part of my soul has gone with him."

—Quincy Jones
Producer of *Thriller*

" One thing Michael did prize, of course, was his single white glove. That was actually my brother Jackie's idea at home one day. He just said, 'You should wear one glove. A white glove.' And then Mike studded it all. That was it."

—Janet Jackson
Musician, producer, actress, Michael's sister

"first album i ever bought was thriller. with birthday money. on cassette. for my brand new sony walkman. truth."

—Mark Hoppus
blink-182, musician, record producer

"I knew Michael as a child and watched him grow over the years. Of all the thousands of entertainers I have worked with, Michael was THE most outstanding. Many have tried and will try to copy him, but his talent will never be matched."

—Dick Clark
Businessman, game show host, radio/television personality

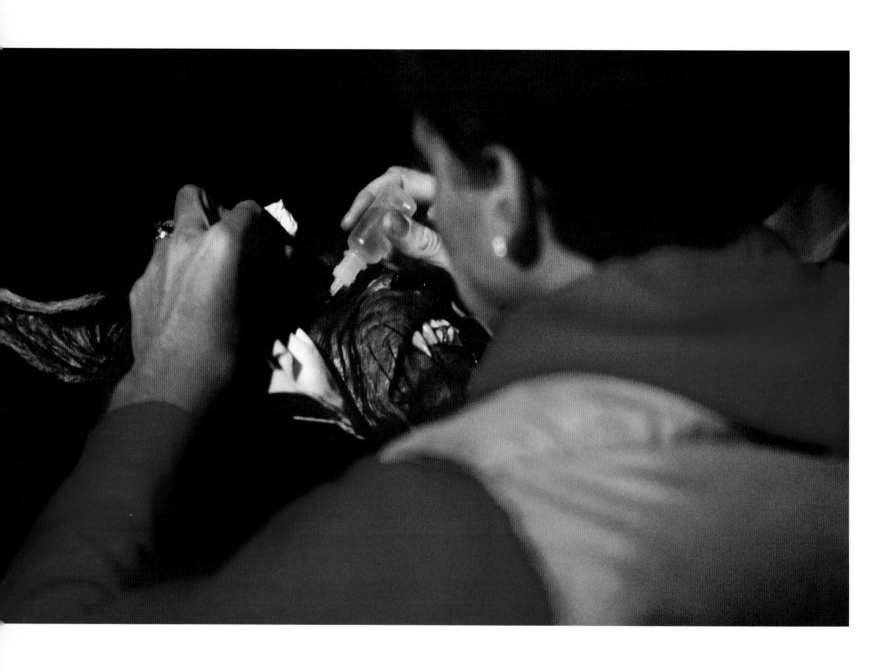

"Everyone thinks I made millions, but I don't care. . . I wouldn't change a thing. The minute I walked into the audition, I knew the part was mine. [Michael] seemed taken by the fact I was a *Playboy* model. He was cute, but childlike. He loved chasing me or jumping out from behind a wall."

—Ola Ray

Model, actress

"If it were not for Michael Jackson I would not be where or who I am today. His music and legacy will live on forever."

—Ludacris
Radio personality, rapper, actor

"I watched a man dance better than anyone I'd ever seen in my life and I watched a man talk softly and carry a tremendously big stick, get what he wanted and get his way. . . I was influenced not only by his talent, but by his personality."

—Bob Giraldi
Director of "Beat It"

"People have found clever ways to make great videos that don't require tons of money. I don't know if we'll ever see another 'Thriller.'"

—Rick Krim
Executive VP of Music and Talent Programming for VH1

"Michael put his heart and soul into his music, his family and into his work of always helping others. . ."

—Tito Jackson
Musician, Michael's brother

" . . . a thousand public voices recount Michael's brilliant, joyous, embattled, enigmatic, bizarre trajectory, [and] I hope the word 'joyous', is the one that will rise from the ashes and shine as he once did."

—Deepak Chopra
Physician, public speaker, writer, philosopher

"He gave me and my family hope. I would never have been me without him."

—MC Hammer
Rapper, actor

Creating the Make-up for
Michael's Zombie

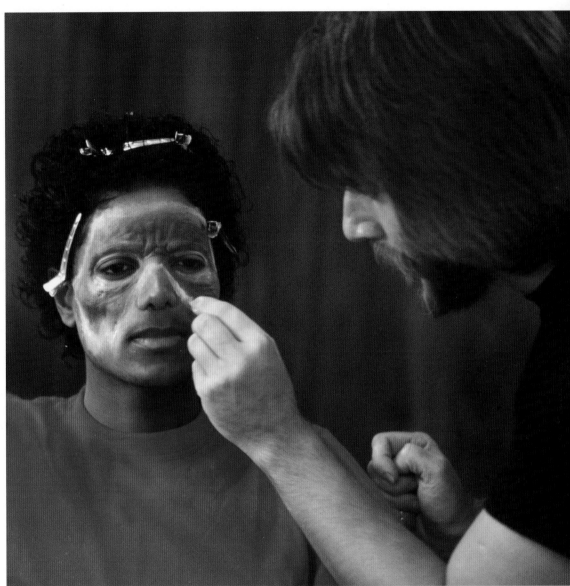

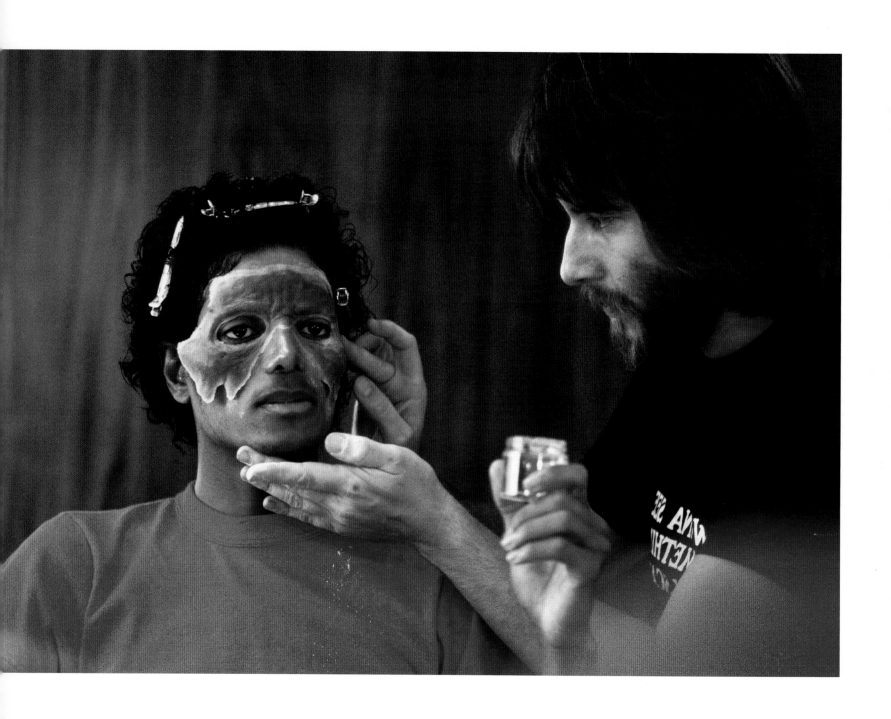

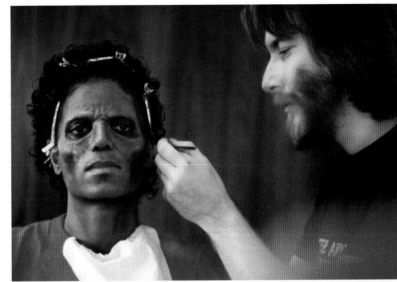
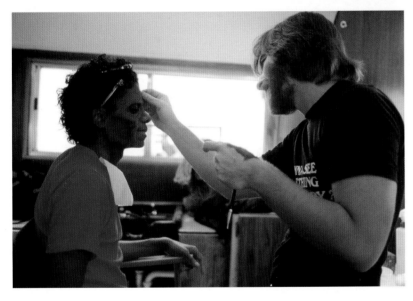

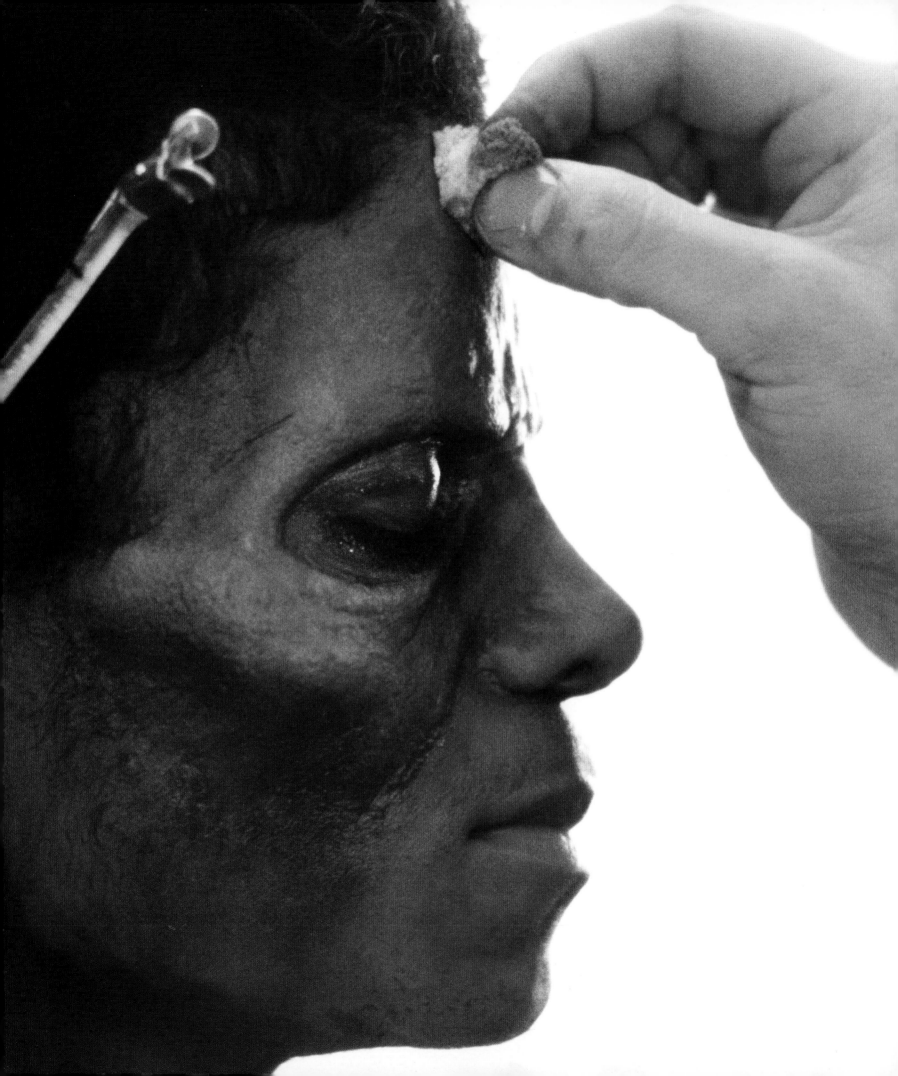

"They doubted me on Michael (Jackson) for *Thriller*. I found the power in being underestimated. It's the greatest place to be."

—Quincy Jones
Producer of *Thriller*

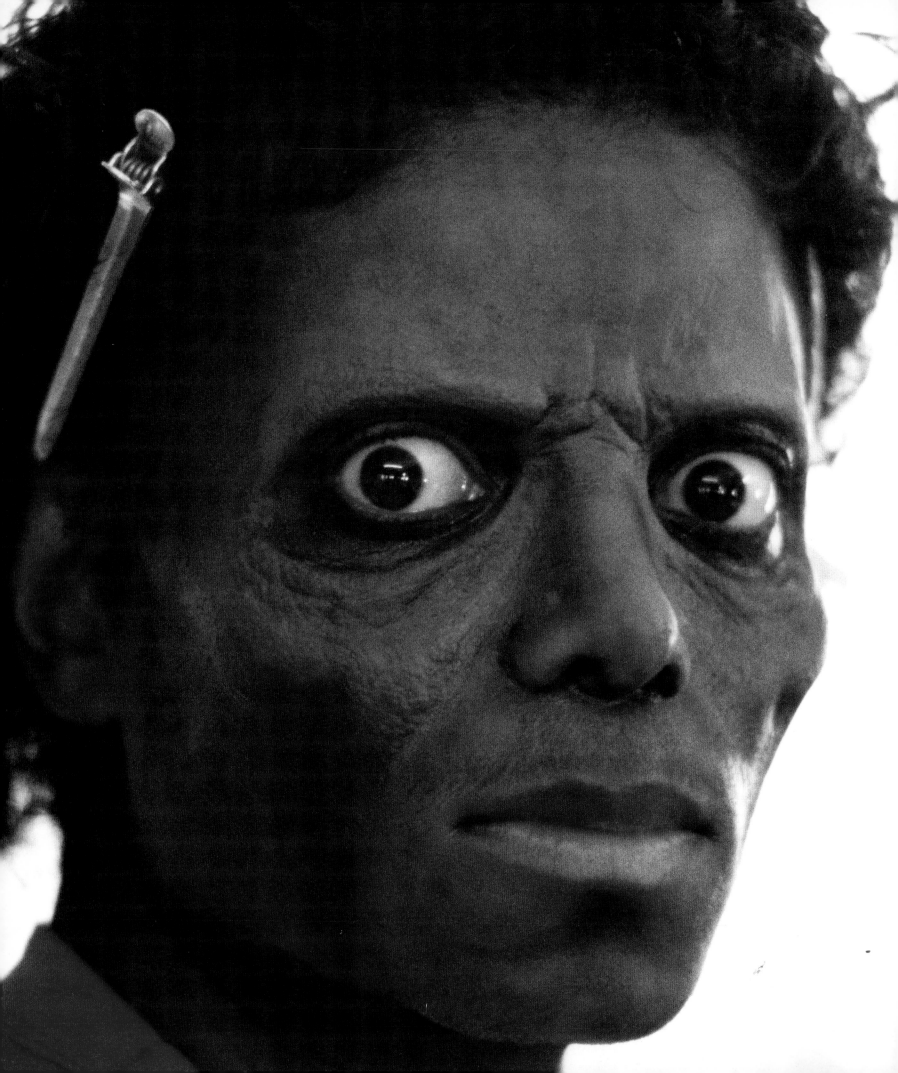

In an interview from the 1980s, published by the *News of the World*, Jackson revealed that he was considering scrapping the *Thriller* album, before being inspired by watching children play to salvage it. He said: "*Thriller* sounded so crap. The mixes sucked. When we listened to the whole album, there were tears. . . I just cried like a baby. I stormed out of the room and said, 'We're not releasing this'." Jackson added: "One of the maintenance crew in the studio had a bicycle and so I took it and rode up to the schoolyard. I just watched the children play. When I came back I was ready to rule the world. I went into the studio and I turned them songs out."

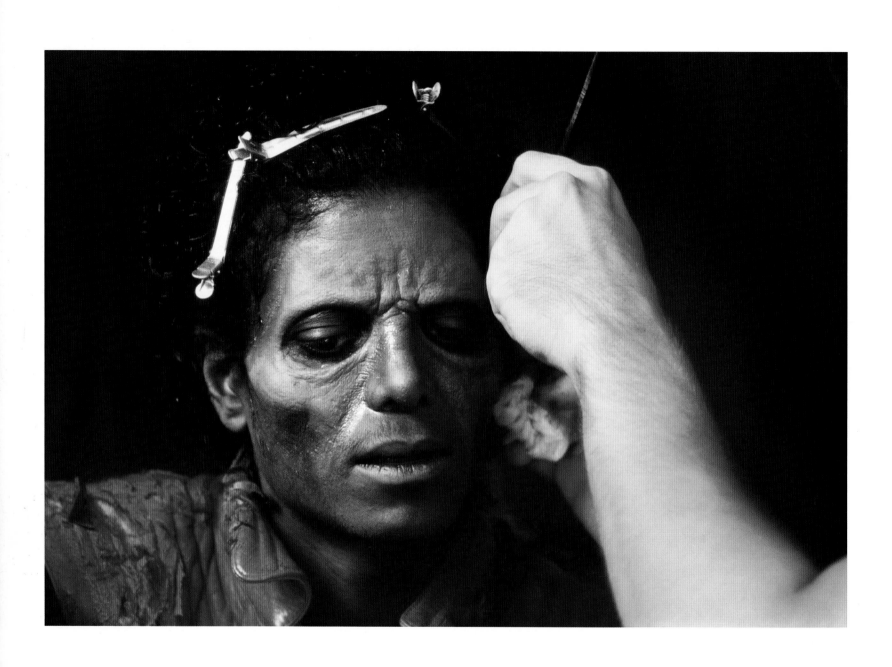

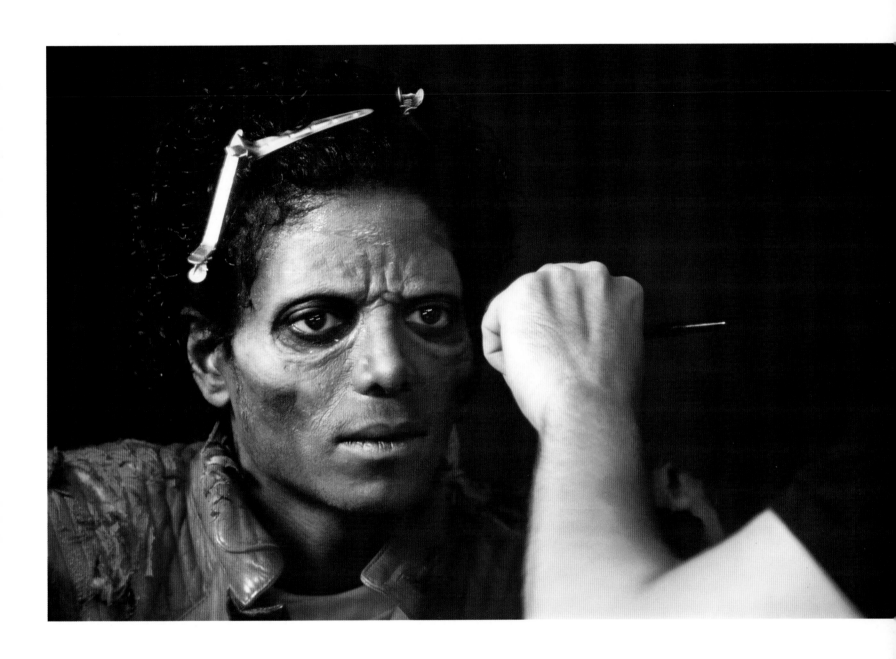

The Abandoned House

"MJ showed me that you can actually see the beat. He made the music come to life!!
He made me believe in magic. . ."

—Diddy
Rapper, record producer, actor and fashion designer

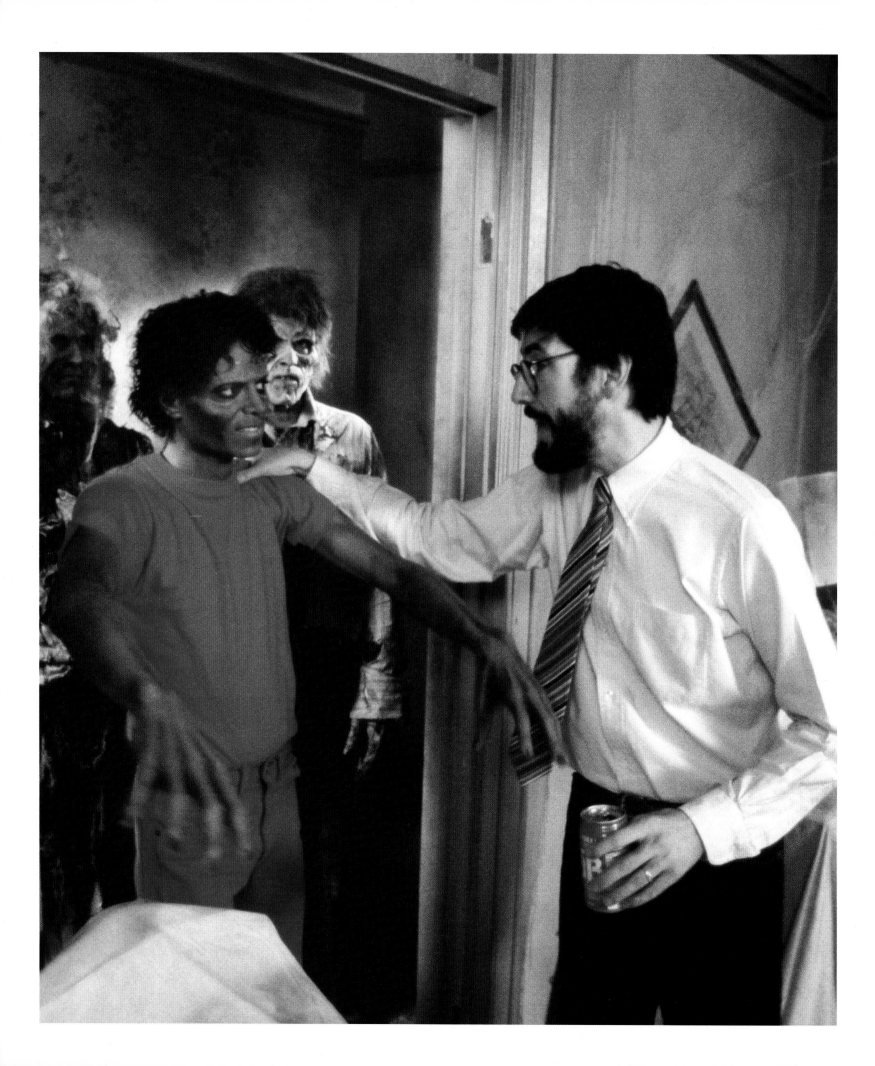

"I personally can't believe it. But it's more unfortunate for the world of music. . .
A sad day in history, not [just] music."

—Lil Wayne
Rapper, actor

" I have to say that I am absolutely a fan of Michael Jackson. He will always be an icon to the world. And I feel like I have always celebrated his genius and his beautiful heart."

—Alicia Keys
Singer-songwriter, record producer, actress, poet,
as interviewed by MTV

"Michael seemed shy, with a quiet disposition, but his dancing was electrifying and had to be seen to be believed. He was just so talented. He was very pleasant and polite—asking me about my family and the other films I had made. Michael was a real movie buff and absolutely loved Disney films. I'm proud to have worked on 'Thriller'—but I'm never totally happy with my work. I can always find things that I would have done differently.

"['Thriller'] was the only time I worked with someone who made me want to write down my thoughts about him and the effect he had on me. As soon as I got back to my hotel room I wrote eight pages on my opinion of MJ! And I still have those notes to this day."

—Robert Paynter
Cinematographer of "Thriller"

"I could measure my childhood until now on an MJ growth chart."

—Pete Wentz
Musician

"'Thriller' ushered in an age of cinematic, high-concept videos. We saw videos get more sophisticated—more story lines, way more intricate choreography. You look at the early videos and they were shockingly bad."

—Nina Blackwood
MTV VJ from 1981 to 1986

Sir Paul McCartney recalled the first time the high-pitched voice of Jackson was on the other end of the phone. The late King of Pop meekly asked him, "'Wanna make some hits?'"—and the result was a pair of smash singles "Say Say Say" and "The Girl is Mine." McCartney called the late "Thriller" singer ". . . a lovely man" and "massively talented." "And we miss him."

Price: When they decided to use me for a series of Poe pictures, I sat down and I read Edgar Allan Poe, and I found out something which I suppose in the back of my mind I'd been told at some time, but I really didn't realize: that about seventy percent of Poe's work is satiric. It is NOT horror. It is not thriller. One that is called "The Sphinx" ends up a very funny thing, and there are a great many of Poe's poems—actually many more than straight Gothic tales—that involve horror, but which also have a comic twist at the end which is alleviating. And this, I decided, should be added to Poe. If I am going to do a Poe picture, I must add that essential twist of Poe's character.

Price: [Pause] I suppose for me—and you always have to talk very personal—to me, I have tried to bring a sense of style to the thrillers that was in one way pseudo, phony, too much, and at the same time based on the audience idea of what it should look like, of what I should look like.

Plath: So these spoofs, then, were really recreation for you?

Price: Absolutely. It was the same reason that I did a thing called "Thriller" with Michael Jackson, which ended up being the biggest-selling album in the business.

Plath: Just for fun?

Price: Right. Just making fun of myself.

—Vincent Price
interview with James Plath, October 3, 2007

"I don't think there will ever be another . . . like it in the history of music. There will never be a marriage of producer and artist, of song writing and pop sensibility like that again. Due to the way people buy records now, there will never be an album that sells as many copies."

—Trevor Nelson
MTV Base overseas digital TV presenter, on *Thriller*

"Michael Peters just wanted great dancers. He was a wonderful choreographer and I think he captured the zombie aspects of the movement really well. His choreography had eclectic rhythms, a sense of humor and a finger on the pulse of what was coming ahead in the world of dance."

—Vincent Peters
Dancer/choreographer's assistant

Vincent Price, while a guest on Johnny Carson's *The Tonight Show*, laughingly stated that when he did the narration for "Thriller" (at the request of Michael Jackson who was a big fan of Price) he had a choice between taking a percentage of the album sales or $20,000. Price was well along in his career, so he took the $20,000. He was good-natured about it when Carson told him he could have made millions off of the royalties due to the vast number of copies sold even at that time. Price laughed heartily and said: "How well I know!"

"'Thriller' does not have the mean, challenging immediacy or weird fervor of a rap record, like 'White Lines.' Michael's got a fresh, original sound. The music is energetic, and it's sensual. You can dance to it, work out to it, make love to it, sing to it. It's hard to sit still to."

—Jane Fonda
Actress, writer

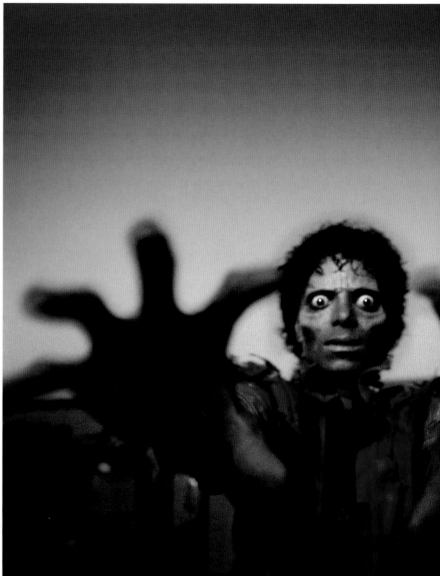

"He actually does radiate an aura when he comes into the studio, there's no question about it. He's not a musician in the sense that Paul is. . . but he does know what he wants in music and he has very firm ideas."

—Sir George Henry Martin
produced the song "Say Say Say" on the *Thriller* album

" . . . I would not be the artist, performer, and philanthropist I am today without the influence of Michael. In so many ways he transcended culture. He broke barriers, he changed radio formats! . . . He made it possible for people like Oprah and Barack Obama to impact the mainstream world. His legacy is unparalleled."

—Usher
Musician, actor, record producer

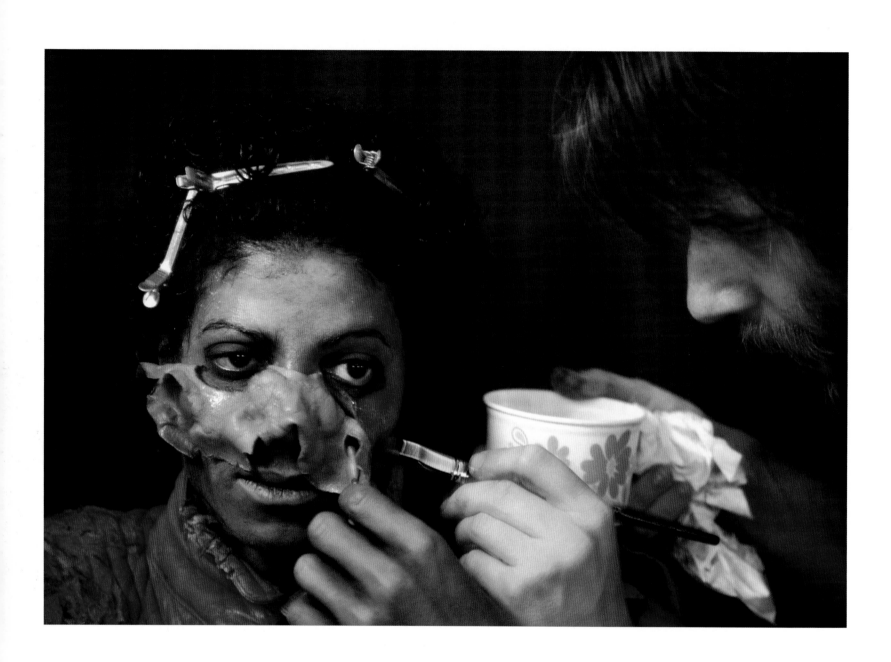

"He has been an inspiration throughout my entire life…"

—Britney Spears
Singer, entertainer, record producer

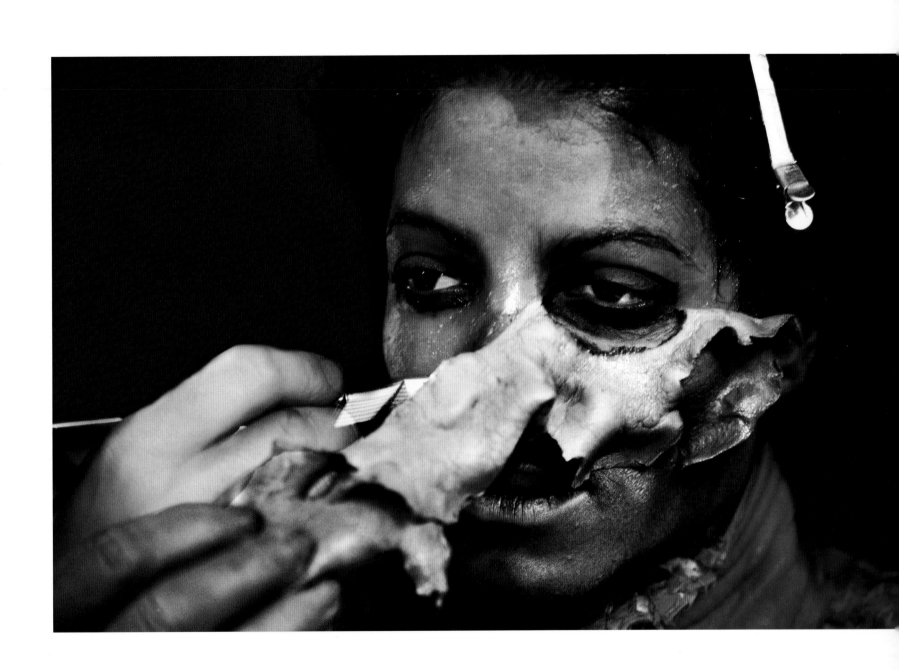

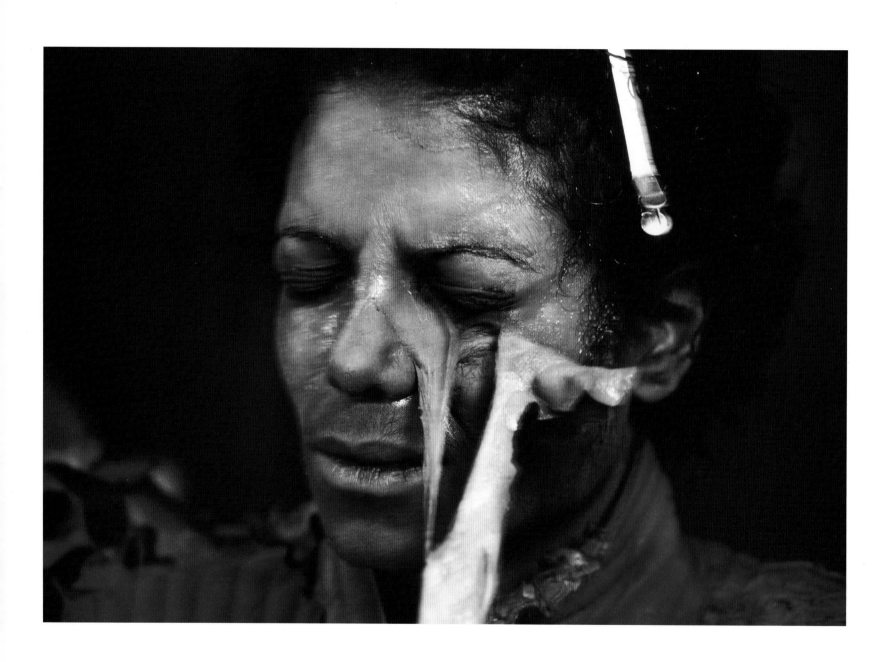

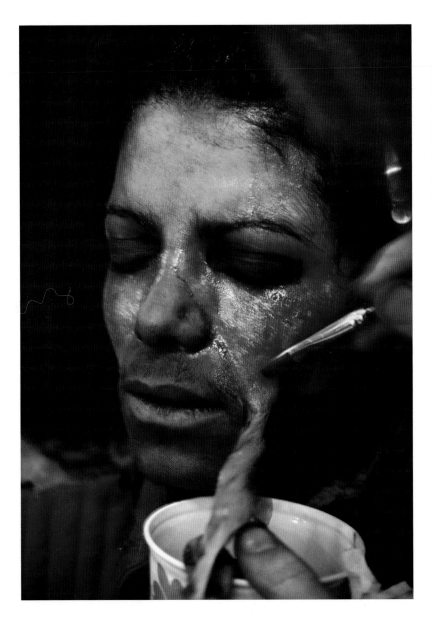

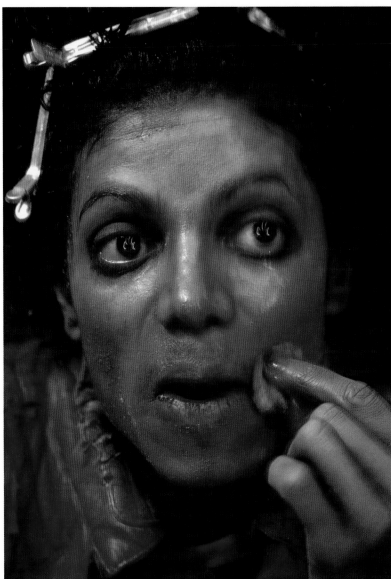

Between Takes: Michael as Himself

"The eternal child, Michael was always friendly and playful between takes. He would hang out with the crew and joke with them, rather than hide in his dressing room."

—Douglas Kirkland

"I remember him calling me and just talking about, you know, 'syncopation' and musician stuff like that. The Michael Jackson I knew was just a musician who loved music."

"He was on my song 'Girls, Girls, Girls,' singing these background vocals and I didn't even put his name on it."

"He played a concert with me in New York, which was great. He got up and he walked out and the place went mental, guys were just grabbing their hats and throwing them like, Aiiiiiiiiieeeeee!"

—Jay-Z
Rapper, entrepreneur

According to "Thriller" director John Landis, Michael was terrific to work with. "He was in his mid-twenties, but he was like a gifted 10-year-old. He was emotionally damaged, but so sweet and so talented." The purpose of *Thriller*, in Landis' mind, was "to give Michael some balls. The making of the video 'Thriller'. . . It was nobody's brilliant idea. I took the job to direct Michael Jackson's landmark music video because I saw it as a chance to resurrect a genre that had once been a Hollywood staple. It was a great opportunity to bring back the theatrical short. Music videos were new in 1983 and MTV was just two years old. At that time the videos were used to sell records and when Michael decided to do the 'Thriller' video, the album had already become the biggest-selling album of all time. It ended up costing $500,000—still enormous money at that time for that kind of thing. Nobody would give us the money, because the album had already been so successful. Michael said he would pay for it, but I wouldn't let him. He was still living with his parents in Encino, behind a supermarket."

George Folsey, Landis' partner in the venture, suggested they make a documentary, to be called, "The Making of "Thriller.'" "We sold that hour to a brand-new thing called cable television and the Showtime Network, which at that time had only three million homes as subscribers. They paid a quarter of a million dollars for the rights to show it exclusively for, I think, ten days." When MTV saw it, they called Landis.

'How can you do that?' they asked.

"We said, 'OK, *you* give us the money.' And they gave us another quarter of a million to show it for two weeks, and that [covered] our costs.'"

"The incomparable Michael Jackson has made a bigger impact on music than any other artist in the history of music. He was magic. He was what we all strive to be. He will always be the King of Pop! Life is not about how many breaths you take, but about how many moments in life that take your breath away. For anyone who has ever seen, felt or heard his art, we are all honored to have been alive in this generation to experience the magic of Michael Jackson. I love you Michael."

—Beyoncé
Singer, record producer, actress

BIOGRAPHIES

Douglas Kirkland

Douglas Kirkland began his career at *Look* and *Life* magazines in the 1960s and 1970s, during the "golden age" of photojournalism. He has worked on the set of more than 100 motion pictures that include such acclaimed productions as *Butch Cassidy and The Sundance Kid, 2001, A Space Odyssey,* and *Out of Africa.* His iconic photographs of Marilyn Monroe and Elizabeth Taylor, among others, are known worldwide. He has authored more than ten books, including the bestseller *James Cameron's Titanic* (HarperCollins); as well as *Freeze Frame: Five Decades/400 Photographs* and *Coco Chanel: Three Weeks/1962* (Glitterati 2007/2009, respectively). His awards include a Lifetime Achievement Award from the American S.O.C., a Lucie for Outstanding Achievement in Entertainment Photography, The Golden Eye of Russia, and a Lifetime Achievement Award from CAPIC in his native Toronto, Canada. In October 2007, Douglas received an Honorary Master of Fine Arts Degree from Brooks Institute.

His work has been exhibited worldwide and his exhibition of the artwork from *Freeze Frame* is in the permanent collection of the American Academy of Motion Picture Arts and Sciences. In September 2008, *Vanity Fair Italy* organized a major retrospective of his work at Milan's Museum of the Triennale. When he is not traveling the globe on assignment with his wife and business partner Françoise, his home and studio is in the Hollywood Hills.

Nancy Griffin

Nancy Griffin is a magazine writer and editor, book author and film producer. An expert on the entertainment industry, her career combines years of covering Hollywood for numerous national publications with experience as a movie executive and producer. Griffin has served as West Coast editor of three national magazines: *AARP The Magazine*, *Premiere* magazine, and *Talk* magazine. She has written extensively about Hollywood for *Vanity Fair*, *The New Yorker*, *Talk*, *Premiere*, *The New York Times*, *Esquire*, *GQ*, *More*, *Newsweek* and *TIME*.

Griffin is the former president of Legende Films, a Los Angeles-based subsidiary of the Paris-based production company Legende ("La Vie En Rose"). She co-produced *Sugar Town,* the 1999 comedy starring Rosanna Arquette and Ally Sheedy, directed by Allison Anders and Kurt Voss, which received an Independent Spirit Award nomination for best feature. She is currently the president of the board of Collage Dance Theater, a non-profit site-specific dance company in Los Angeles.

Griffin is co-author with Kim Masters of *The New York Times* 1995 bestseller *Hit and Run: How Jon Peters and Peter Guber took Sony for a Ride in Hollywood*. She lives in Venice, CA with her husband, the architect Steven Ehrlich.

ACKNOWLEDGMENTS

This book is the brainchild of our outstanding publisher, Marta Hallett, and driven by her boundless enthusiasm. Once again, Sarah Morgan Karp's sensitive design and pacing has turned this into a jewel, of which I am very proud. I feel fortunate to have had a long friendship with Nancy Griffin through our years of working together; her contribution to this project is priceless. Miranda Brackett, Jeremy Oversier and Will Thoren, in our studio, each worked tirelessly to put the images together. My family, my friends, my Françoise—everyone needs a Françoise— thank you all for your love and support. You keep me inspired!